Late-in-Life Lesbian

BY SHELBY THEVENOT

SHELBY THEVENOT

Copyright © 2024 Shelby Thevenot

All rights reserved.

ISBN: 978-1-7381396-0-6

Cover design by Shelby Thevenot
Photos of opening night by Brooklyn Melnyk

Performance Rights:
All performance rights to this play are controlled exclusively by Shelby Thevenot or their authorized agent. No performance of this play may be given without obtaining in advance the written permission of Shelby Thevenot or their authorized agent, and paying the required royalty fee.

Royalties:
The royalty fee for each performance of this play is $10, payable to Shelby Thevenot or their authorized agent. This fee is due prior to the performance date.

Contact for permissions and royalties:
shelbythevenot.com/contact

Late-in-Life Lesbian

Trigger warnings:

Sexual violence, death, homophobia

Late-in-Life Lesbian

The world premiere of *Late-in-Life Lesbian* was part of the 34th edition of the St-Ambroise Montreal FRINGE Festival where it received an honourable mention for the Frankie Award for English Comedy. The original production was directed by Lucy Gervais, and was showcased at Petit Campus in Tiohtià:ke (a.k.a. Montreal) for six performances between June 8 and June 16, 2024.

Late-in-Life Lesbian

CAST

- Shelby
- Gay Voice

The two characters may be played by the same actor.

PRODUCTION NOTES

- The set requires a fruit platter containing at least one grapefruit, and a surface on which to put said platter.
- Producers, directors, and performers are invited to deviate from the original script as required by audience response. Music choices of the original production are kept in the script for historical records but are not mandatory for every production.
- Please ensure all trigger warnings of sexual violence, death, and homophobia are clearly visible to patrons.

Late-in-Life Lesbian

Late-in-Life Lesbian

Dedicated to all late-in-life queers and those who love them.

LATE-IN-LIFE LESBIAN

[Lights up on a stage with a table of fruit. Shelby enters accompanied by music: Pretty Girls Walk by Big Boss Vette.]

SHELBY

Hello Tiohtià:ke, Montreal, how are we all doing tonight?

I really appreciate you guys coming out to hear my little story about coming out. That's right, I am a lesbian and I'm also non-binary.

You might have guessed by the title of this show called, "Late-in-Life Lesbian" that it would be gay as hell. Did any straight people come out anyway? Hey! Thanks for coming out.

I never heard of late-in-life lesbians until it turned out I was one. I kind of thought if you were gay you always knew you always just felt a certain way. Maybe you saw Kate Winslet in literally any movie and you were like, "Huh..."

[Point to imaginary TV then point to self.]

"Gay."

I came out at age 32. And since then I've met many late-in-life lesbians who came out at ages all over the place: 34, 36, 43—*62*— It's an epidemic.

It's so bad whenever someone tells me they're

straight I feel it's my right and my duty to say:

"ARE YOU SURE?!"

I don't think there's a particular age where you can start calling yourself a late-in-life lesbian, but I'm pretty sure that it has to be at a time when people stop asking "How did you know you were gay?" and they start asking "How did you *not* know you were gay?"

Well, I'll tell you. I grew up in the woods.

I grew up outside a small town called Portage la Prairie. Where if you listened closely you could hear the sound of dinner.

[Cow sound effect]

If you don't know where Portage la Prairie is, it's a town in Manitoba.

And if you don't know where Manitoba is, well it's a province in Canada. It's known for the Winnipeg Jets, which is a hockey team, the Crash Test Dummies, which is a band—and it's also known for murder. And I don't wanna brag but, last I checked my town had the third most murders per capita in the country. One famous one involved a beheading on a Greyhound bus.

The joke around town after that happened was: "Hey, did you hear about Greyhound's new slogan? We be going where you beheaded."

When I look back on Manitoba, I love it a lot

more now that I'm older. It's a lot like going to bed at nine o'clock in that way.

Manitoba's so small that it's not unusual to meet somebody who knows you—or at least somebody who knows somebody who knows you. And if you were to say I dunno, be a lesbian — they'd know that too.

That's not just small news man. That is hot gossip. I remember being told a story by my aunt, "Do you remember Rachel Polinski? Well — she divorced her second husband and last I heard she's dating a lady now." Like it was a bad thing. Like this person had failed to find a man. And the take-away was: you fail to find man, you fail at life.

As a young, non-binary person growing up as a "girl." You're also told that the best day of your life is going to be your wedding day. Then once you have a baby—you did it. You have won womanhood. Now you can die.

I grew up in a very sex-negative environment. I learned about sex when I was I was ten years old. I was reading the Children's Encyclopedia and it said that sex is when the penis goes into the vagina— and the point of it all is to get the penis to ejaculate. Because that's how you win. Because jizz is such a prize.

And after I learned all this I told all my friends. I became the class sex ed teacher. It was between our gym teacher, Mr. Lang, who didn't want to be there, or me, who was chubby and awkward and reading books had finally made me popular.

And I will admit, I probably wasn't a very good sex ed teacher. I thought sex was just P and V, which is as bad as thinking that sandwiches are just P, B, and J.

And when you grow up in an environment where the best sex ed teacher in school is YOU it's like — "Well, how did you not know you were a lesbian?" It's like—nobody asked! Including me. THE SEX ED TEACHER.

I wasn't the only bad sex ed teacher. I can't say sex ed is very good in Manitoba—or anywhere, really. They don't tell you human sexuality and gender are fluid and complex. Nah. Sex ed is just a banana and a condom.

The only thing I knew about "the gays" at that time was whatever the straight people in my life told me about them and whatever I saw on TV. And I had six channels, and one of them was Fox News— and that was back when Fox News *had* trash comedy cartoons and before it *became* one.

I'll tell you when I was a kid information was not as easily accessible.

[Sound Cue: Good, Bad, and Ugly Theme.]

Back in my day, there was no high-speed internet. There was no GooGoo, or TikTok, or Instagram. We had dial-up internet, a phone with a cord, and a fax machine—and you couldn't use two of those things at the same time.

It wasn't only the technology but civil rights weren't even the same. Same-sex marriage was legalized in Manitoba when I was 13 years old. And that means all the adults in my life and the children I grew up with had never known a world where same-sex marriage was legal. So by then, I was already homophobic. Not everyone in Manitoba was. But I was.

One of my lifelong best friends is a lesbian. Her name is Ann. We grew up in the same place, she came out at age 15. The other day we were talking about why I came out later in life. She told me, "You know, I don't think it's just the environment we grew up in. I think it's you."

Right? My best fucking friend.

She said, "I think you just care too much about what other people think."

And that's very true.

In high school, I was a good Christian girl. I was a cheerleader. I was a cheerleader who deep down was a cynical closeted lesbian, who dressed like a goth chick and said homophobic shit for Jesus.

And that's not a great thing to admit especially as today, not only am I a homosexual—I'm also an atheist. And I have been for some time.

God is not real. But if he was, he'd be a lesbian.

And the punishment for being homophobic would be 13 years of bad sex and following it up with lesbian dating in your 30s where you have no sex.

[Hang head in self-pity.]

So, hopefully, by now you probably get why I didn't really come out of the closet, until a bit later. I was successfully brainwashed. Somewhat willfully because it's a good view you know when you're a non-binary lesbian sitting at the straight white lady's table. If you just ignore the constant screaming in your head—

GAY VOICE

GET ME OUT OF HERE!!!!—Hey! YOU!!!!

[Shelby points to themself.]

GAY VOICE

You would be so much happier if you were a lesbian!

SHELBY

Yeah, that's what the gay thoughts sound like. And old Shelby would just—

[Shelby covers their ears.]

GAY VOICE

Oh, come on man. Can't you be just a little bit bi,

even?

SHELBY

But if you can ignore the screaming—and tell those gay thoughts that, no, in fact drawing a picture of a naked Greek goddess in an iHop is completely heterosexual behaviour (it was Aphrodite), and if you can get used to not looking yourself in the mirror—you can cover up your personality with somebody else's and you can live a pretty good life.

But it does bring us to the follow-up question. After the people want to know, "How did you not know you were gay," they want to know, "How did you find out? What made you come out of the closet?"

Well, my coming out story starts as any good story starts. I dumped my boyfriend. Thank you. And you know what? He wasn't even a boyfriend. He was more of a fiancé.

Yeah. Why don't we say his name was Ned. It's a good name. Rhymes with Ted.

So, I started dating Ned. One month later we moved in together. Four months later got engaged. A few months after that I dumped him. Bought a car. Took all my stuff out of his house. Drove across the country. Brought him with me. Dumped him again.

That's the short version. We'll get into some more details later.

Needless to say, it wasn't my shining ten months. I U-Hauled with a man.

But to understand why I did that, you have to know that the person I was when I was with him is not the same person I am today. And it's not the same person I was before the pandemic, either.

My life changed in June 2020, the height of the pandemic. I was living alone working from home. Everyone in the world was freaking out. At that time there was no treatment for COVID. No vaccine. Just lots of people sick and dying. And there was me, so sick, lying on my bathroom floor.

I was alone. And I thought, "I'm gonna die here. On my bathroom floor."

I called 9-11. And when the ambulance arrived I had no idea if or when I would be coming home from the hospital.

I was in there for three days. I got to spend a night in the COVID ward. It was like being a hamster at the pet store. There were three white walls and one that was plexiglass where you could see all the healthcare professionals running around inside.

You could hear screaming in the room next to you—

GAY VOICE

HEY! I KNOW WHAT YOU THINK ABOUT IN THE NIGHT!

SHELBY

—and one of the healthcare workers says, "We've done all we can do," and you're like, "What does that mean?"

GAY VOICE

THERE ARE HOMOSEXUAL THOUGHTS COURSING THROUGH YOUR MIND. LET THEM FLOW!!!!

SHELBY

And then suddenly the screaming stops!

[Gay Voice gets cut off. Shelby shrugs.]

And then you have to pee and there is a commode in your room that's got a plastic bag in it. So you pee in the bag and you gotta knock on the plexiglass like a kid at the aquarium to get one of the healthcare fishes to come over and take your pee bag away. Forget about pooping. You hold that shit in.

And of course, they ask you all the pink questions. Which I understand why, but it's still kinda funny.

They're like, "Any chance you're pregnant?"

"No."

"We'll test ya anyway."

Why did you ask then? Just take the pee bag. I don't care what you do with it.

"Are you sure it's not your period."

"Yes, I'm sure… because if it was… I'd be on my period."

Then finally they go, "OK. You really are sick."

Well that's good news man! Because that's why I'm here, actually.

It turns out I didn't have COVID.

[Pick up grapefruit from fruit platter.]

I had what's called an ovarian cyst. It was the size of a grapefruit. If a grapefruit is 11x12x8 cm.

I was told I'd have to get surgery to remove it. I've never had surgery before.

And you know, my mind always goes to the worst-case scenario so I can prepare for it. Like a squirrel collecting negative thoughts for the winter. Filling those little cheeks, "I'm gonna die."

So a few months later, I walked into that

operating room it was very much like something you would see on TV. It was metallic, it had one operating table in the centre that was shaped like the outline of police tape around a dead body.

And as I laid down I tried not to show my fear. Because I was scared. I laid down on the operating table and I think, "Well, this is it." And I let out a sigh. And my anesthesiologist says, "Oh, I know that sigh." And he puts the gas mask on my face and he says, "You're gonna be OK. You're gonna be OK."

And that was the last thing I heard before I went to sleep.

[Return grapefruit to platter.]

And if by some freak accident, I wouldn't have made it out of that surgery, the last thing I would have heard on this earth was, "You're gonna be OK. You're gonna be OK."

So it's like, for a cynical lesbian, maybe being delulu is the selulu. Sometimes.

I woke up and my stomach was flat. It was like night and day. But recovery was tough. For the first few days I couldn't even walk from my front door to my sidewalk, it's like two steps. I had to have friends stay with me. And the whole experience really gave me a sense of urgency like I really cannot be single anymore. I really need somebody to help take care of me when I'm sick. I don't wanna die alone on my bathroom floor. I really have to find my person. Now.

So, I'll always remember 2021 as the year of terrible dates. One man even slapped me. Yeah. On the first date. And that's only my second-worst date ever.

Sometimes, I bring up this story in its short form, hoping it's enough. Just like, "Y'know, men are shit. One guy slapped me on the first date."

But this one guy I told kinda pissed me off. He goes, "What's the context?"

Now, in most contexts, it's good to know the context. And, I did cry for 12 hours after, so I'm quite certain I've earned the right to bitch.

But this guy— we'll call him Chuck. It's a good name. Rhymes with "truck". Chuck wants to know if I deserved it.

So, I tell him: I went on a date with this man, his name was Slappy, rhymes with crappy—I should have known.

We get into bed. We start having sex. And it's awful. He's all like, "Stop making noise you'll make me cum," and I'm like, isn't that the point? To make you stop? Or am I just a closeted lesbian?

He's the one making noises like a dog, but I don't say anything. And then he stops and says, "Hey, can I slap you?"

Now, what he was looking for in that moment

was an excited and enthusiastic, "Fuck yes."

What he got was, "OK. Sure. Let's try it."

And as a former sex ed teacher, I can confirm—and four out of five dentists would agree—Those. Are not. The same. Thing.

But he slapped me anyway.

And I lied there kinda stunned. I had just been slapped on the face.

And what I was looking for was a check-in. "Hey, did you like that?"

What he was looking for was a, "Do it again, Slappy!"

But neither of those things happened, and he slapped me again anyway.

Now, back to Chuck. Sitting there, thoughtfully rubbing his chin, points at me to say.

"But you did say, yes."

He continues.

"You see what happens, when you have the full context. Suddenly, it doesn't seem so bad."

So, fuck Chuck.

"What's the context?" What's the context for you, sir?

Anyway, after a year of terrible dates, still in this mindset of "I HAVE to find somebody"— I meet Ned.

I knew Ned from before, but not very well. I knew he was into meditation. I wanted to learn about meditation. So our first "date" was not really a date. We were just supposed to meditate. I don't really know what I'm getting into but Ned brings me to this church and we go in the basement and the first thing I see is against the far wall, six pictures of dudes in a line. One of them is Krishna, one of them is white Jesus, and I don't recognize the other four.

And I'm not saying that it's bad if that sort of thing fills your spiritual cup, I'm just saying, athiestly speaking, I'd rather do anything else. I'd get a better spiritual experience from touching a tree. We're different and that's beautiful.

So, I told Ned afterwards, "I had a good meditation, but I don't think I'd like to go back ever again."

Well, you can probably guess how that turned out.

We ended up spending the whole day together. And then before I knew it we were dating. And it was good. And I did go back to that place. Many, many times.

I did many things that I didn't want to do in order to make Ned happy, but he still found new and creative ways to get pissed at me. I'd list them all, but we'd be here forever.

Some of my favourites though: wearing shorts, eating chicken, looking at a pool.

And literally, any interaction with any man ever— didn't matter if he was gay, in a relationship, or delivering Uber Eats. I'd call him a man-hating lesbian but that is a compliment he does not deserve.

But it was so hard to leave him.

Ned was actually so sweet. He showered me with gifts. He drew me pictures. He proposed to me by editing a short clip into the movie we were watching. I don't remember which one, though.

And he'd do sweet stuff like that but then he'd go and do scary stuff. Like how after he gave the ring he says: "I got my buddy in Madagascar who mines gemstones to bring a bunch of people on a very dangerous expedition to get you the perfect ring. But, I wasn't happy with what he got so I bought this on Etsy."

[Shelby looks freaked out.]

And I'd be like, "Aww. How romantic."

I mean, I'd be happy with a ring pop from the right person.

But at least with him I had somebody. With him I wouldn't die alone. I may have even had a hope in hell of having a family. With a home and kids.

And of course, while all this was happening, my male gynecologist was telling me, "Better hurry up and have kids or you are never gonna have any."

And I was like—OK, that's a terrible thing to tell someone whose fertility is compromised. I know this is just a normal day for you but this is the rest of my fucking life, sir.

And it's not that I ever really wanted to have kids. And despite that whole thing about having kids to win womanhood— I didn't really tie my gender identity to being a mother. But as soon as I was faced with *never* having kids suddenly the stakes were enormous. "Never" is so final. And I didn't have any say in it.

And Ned wanted kids, but when he was mad he was scary. And at one point, while he was screaming, my dog—she's a little beagle.

She comes to sit on my lap. She's so scared she's shaking. And I look down at her, and all I see is my future. Being the mother of children with this man…and them looking to me to save them… and I don't know how.

So I left. And it was the hardest thing I ever had to do. I never want to be in that situation ever again.

So after it was all done, I finally asked myself questions I never asked myself before. Difficult questions about what I want out of life and love. Who am I really? Not who do people want me to be. Who am I? Am I the type of person who puts the toilet paper roll with the end facing the outside? Or, do I like to make things more difficult for everyone? When I'm walking in the street, and I see someone coming toward me, do I move over to let them pass? Or, do I keep barreling forward and expect them to move? And if they don't, when we bump into each other, do I say, "Sorry, excuse me?" Or do I say, "Watch where you're going!"

WHO AM I?

The gender thing came first. I've always felt that I'm not quite a woman, and probably a lot of my elementary peers would agree. They used to call me "The Man Girl." Which was mean at the time but now it's kinda affirming.

My gender identity is still a journey, but these days I go by "butch." And no one needed to give me permission for that. That's just how I feel.

One day, I asked my lesbian friend, Ann, to call me by they/them pronouns, just as an experiment. So, she pretended like she was introducing me to somebody new. She said: "This is my friend Shelby, they are very cool!" I thought, wow—that's so badass. So it stuck.

When it came to questioning my sexuality, I took note of the fact that I never needed sex the way my friends did. Gay or straight I just felt that they all had this drive that I never had. So, I thought maybe, maybe I'm asexual. But, kind of a slutty asexual. One that—maybe wanted sex like once per year, in missionary. I could either be straight, but a bit prudy or I could be asexual but a bit slutty. And I wanted to be a slut.

But then the next step was thinking well, if I don't have to have sex with anyone— then that means I can date everyone! So I was saying on the dating apps that I was greysexual and panromantic.

But then I noticed I was only swiping on women and non-binary folks. And then TikTok, of all people, asks me, "Are you sure you're asexual? Or are you just gay?"

So I watched lesbian porn.

[Music cue: Circle of Life from The Lion King]

And let me tell you...I was like a fourteen-year-old boy discovering boobies for the first time. It was—some people's gay awakening is Xena Warrior Princess, mine was: [Lesbian] The best sex with love using a lover and a double-headed dildo.

It was after that I finally said the words out loud, "I am a lesbian." And it was like a huge weight had been lifted off my shoulders. For a second I thought, "Oh my god...Have I cured my depression?" Is lesbian porn the cure for depression? It's not but— it can be.

                GAY VOICE
HEY!

                SHELBY
Hey.

                GAY VOICE

You know something?! I'm proud of you.

                SHELBY
You too.

When I was an "ally" I didn't realize homophobia went both ways. You can be homophobic to other people, but you can also be homophobic toward yourself. You can say, "I want the best for the gays. I want every queer person to live their best life. I don't wanna be gay though." And that's still homophobia.

And you know what else happened when I was an ally, I participated in a study on human arousal. Yeah. I got paid to watch porn.

They make you fill out a questionnaire and ask you about what kind of shit you're into. Then they lube up this little device— looks like a tampon but it has a light on it— like a little pussy lighthouse. And then you shove it up your vagina and you sit on a medical exam table with a fuzzy blanket over you—they want to make it feel like home. Pretty sure there was a fake plant in the corner, and the walls were painted a brown colour that probably had an appropriate paint name like, "beaver brown" or "hardwood" or something. "Scat party." I'm just making shit up.

And then they put porn on the TV. And they also play boring shit like B-roll of a village in Switzerland, and you have to rate how horny you feel on a scale of 1 to 10.

What they found from that study is that vaginas will respond to sexual images even if the people who own them don't report being aroused. Penises though... they know what's up.

[Grab grapefruit.]

Like if your testicle had a grapefruit growing out of it you would know.

You'd probably even know before it got to that point.

[Put grapefruit back.]

But that's not to suggest that our friends with dicks always know how they feel in the moment. Maybe they can't put a word to it. And even if they could, people in general don't always say how they're really feeling, because it's not always safe.

When someone on the upper end of a power dynamic, like a boss, a teacher, a family member —or even not, even just someone you thought you trusted— puts their hand on you... and you just kinda just smile.

[Smile big.]

Because it's safer to smile even though you're screaming inside. And you just let it happen.

Because you know if you say anything you become the one "causing" the issue.

So it's safer to smile.

I smiled like that for 32 years while I was in the closet. I'm not smiling like that anymore.

I came out after a particularly traumatic breakup up and maybe some people will think, "Oh, it was the breakup that made this person gay. They're just sick of men."

And yes, but—

Trauma does not make you gay. That is a lie rooted in conversion therapy.

Trauma keeps us in the closet.

And for some of us, it's the big one. Maybe you know what I'm talking about.

There are many ways a teenage girl might respond to something like that.

And one way is to distance yourself from it by having partner after partner, creating layers of new experiences to hide the old. And it doesn't matter if you like it or not. Because nothing could be more disgusting than the first time.

"What's the context?"

The context is we live in a world that cares more about a man's reputation than a little girl's bodily autonomy. That is the context, sir.

And when you strip that from her in a world that hates women and gays and convince her that she is only ever expected to marry a man you get a late-in-life lesbian, sir.

This is a comedy show, we might have flipped to the other side of the coin, for a moment. But we'll be right back.

Being a late-in-life lesbian is not a failure. If anything, it's a victory.

I was so scared of how I would die, I didn't care about how I would live.

The truth is most people die alone anyway. Probably, of a horrible chronic disease. Or maybe suddenly. You might have just bought groceries. You might have got them ordered for delivery. Pressed, "Buy now" and said, "What a time to be alive!" Boom. Dead. Marriage is not necessarily going to save you from that.

One of the last things my ex said to me after I dumped him was, "But who would love you?

[Sad face.]

Who would love you?"

First of all, fucking anyone but you. But mostly, me.

I've had to make peace with the fact that I might never be a parent and I might never find love. But it's better to be alone than to be with someone who does not make you feel safe and self-actualized.

I am learning to set boundaries, and be consistent, and caring. I decide how I live, and eat, and dress. And I will look at any damn pool I want to.

I used to care so much about what other people think. I would bend into unrecognizable shapes of myself to get people to like me, but were any of those people there beside me when I thought I was going to die on my bathroom floor? No.

The only one who was, was the person I had been up until that point.

So now, I'm going to live my life so that when I die alone I'll at least like the person who is dying with me.

And I may be just a little bit delulu, but I don't really believe that I'll never find love—unless I get hit by a bus tomorrow or something.

Remember the 62-year-old late-in-life lesbian? I know her from Facebook. She made this comment, she said: "I think it's too late for me to be a lesbian."

And of course, you understand why she'd feel that way, but it's not true. You can find love at any age. There's no wrong time. It's never too late to be a lesbian.

I've met many late-in-life lesbians who came out at ages all over the place—34, 36, 43, 62—it's an epidemic.

And I believe all of them will find love. And if I can believe in them, I can believe in me.

[Lights down. Lights up on music cue: Good Life by One Republic.]

PHOTOS OF WORLD PREMIERE

ACKNOWLEDGEMENTS

Special thanks are in order to Lucy Gervais, the original director of *Late-in-Life Lesbian*, not only for their aspirational talent and creativity, but for showing me kindness and friendship throughout this process. Special thanks also to Nat Pace, who introduced me to Lucy when I was looking for a director; Lou Laurence, who helped me tremendously with making merch and showing me the ropes of Fringe; Sandi Armstrong who helped workshop an earlier version of the script, Amy Blackmore for her leadership, and to all the sponsors of the world premiere production.

I'd also like to thank the people who were directly involved in helping me through the period of my life that this show is based on. Leonard and Anne Thevenot, who showed me great hospitality during my time of need. My dad, John Thevenot, who makes me feel safe like no other. Jani Sorensen, my aunt who went above and beyond to promote the show, even though she was thousands of kilometres away in Manitoba. All six of my grandparents—Grant and Marilyn Sorensen, Paul and Ruth Thevenot, Brenda Bond and Don Gabel—who always hold a special place in my heart. And of course, the friends who were directly involved in helping me through this: Cailin Woodward, Carl Cloutier, Megan Amstutz, Kyle Spreadbury, and Ann Kirschman.

And of course my comedic inspirations, Hannah Gadsby and Mike Birbiglia for through your works I learned the art of comedic storytelling.

Late-in-Life Lesbian is dedicated to all queers who came out later in life, and those who are questioning. We may have vastly different stories, reasons for being closeted, and chains of events that lead us to come out, but I hope there's at least a kernel in my story that affirms and validates your experience.

Lastly, thanks to you, dear reader, for picking up this little script. It's been a lifetime in the making and I sincerely hope you've enjoyed it.

—Shelby

ABOUT THE PLAYWRIGHT

Shelby Thevenot (they/them) is a Canadian writer, poet, playwright, stand-up comedian, journalist and copywriter. *Late-in-Life Lesbian* is their breakout solo show and it was nominated with an honourable mention for the Frankie Award for English Comedy at the 2024 Montreal FRINGE Festival. Shelby's plays and sketch comedies have been featured in Montreal Sketch Fest in Montreal, as well as the Chinook Regional One Act Festival and at the David Spinks Theatre in Lethbridge, Alberta. Their chapbook, *Growing Pains* is available on Amazon.

MORE BOOKS BY SHELBY THEVENOT

Growing Pains by Shelby Thevenot is a book of poems about resilience, living with intergenerational trauma, and growing up.

Buy it on Amazon

www.ingramcontent.com/pod-product-compliance
Lightning Source LLC
Chambersburg PA
CBHW052207070526
44585CB00017B/2109